# AMERICAN
# MOTOCROSS
ILLUSTRATED

## V O L U M E   2

Photos By Simon Cudby

Captions By Davey Coombs

Profiles By Eric Johnson

Design By David Langran

The American motocross and supercross circuit is the most competitive, prestigious and lucrative in the off-road world. As a result, it attracts the very best talent from all over the sport. Top riders from motocross hotbeds such as France, Australia, Costa Rica and South Africa line up on the starting gate to challenge the best riders the United States of America has to offer. While the American circuit is considered a "national" one by definition, it could be argued that the U.S. tours are the true world championships of supercross and motocross racing. (In the case of supercross, it really was part of a world championship, as two races in Europe preceded the 16 rounds held in the United States as part of the FIM/THQ World Supercross GP tour.)

The 2003 THQ/AMA Supercross Series began at Edison International Field in Anaheim, California, to a packed house. This was the very same building which held the seventh game of the 2002 World Series just two months earlier, and the energy and enthusiasm was just as intense for supercross as it was for Major League Baseball. Adding to the drama was the startling news that Jeremy McGrath, the all-time King of Supercross, had decided to retire right before the season-opener. As a result, the series would be considered Jeremy's "Farewell Tour," as well as a preview of what supercross will look like in the years to come.

Team Honda's Ricky Carmichael, the two-time defending series champion, was the overwhelming pre-race favorite going into the opener, but the Floridian has a love-hate relationship with California and the Anaheim crowd. He once again failed to deliver an opening round win after a bad start and two early crashes. Instead of Carmichael, it was Australian Yamaha rider Chad Reed who scored the victory, setting the tone for a series filled with upsets and surprises.

Every Saturday night from January through May, crowds of 50,000 or more packed into stadiums to see the Carmichael-Reed duel. Along the way, the fans were also treated to a couple of fantastic championship battles in 125cc Regional Supercross racing. In the West, James "Bubba" Stewart dazzled the fans with his skill and charisma, winning all but one of the races on his Kawasaki KX125. It was a different story in the East, as Suzuki's Branden Jesseman bat-

tled back against the likes of veterans Mike Brown and Brock Sellards, as well as Sellards' Yamaha of Troy teammate Ivan Tedesco. But when the big East-West Shootout took place in Las Vegas at the end of the season, it was little-known Coloradoan Andrew Short of the MotoworldRacing.com Suzuki team who emerged from the carnage as the upset winner.

In the 250cc class, Carmichael was fighting for his crown. After following up his loss at the opener by winning seven of the next nine races, Carmichael seemed to start going backwards. Instead of running the table as he had done in his two previous title bids, RC was relegated to second behind the phenomenal Reed, who reeled off six straight wins to end the series. Fortunately for Carmichael, the series ended in Las Vegas, with Reed still seven points behind him.

From Las Vegas, the teams went directly to San Bernardino, California, for the opening round of the 2003 AMA/Chevy Trucks National Motocross Championships. Carmichael was back in charge in his more comfortable outdoor surroundings, and within three weeks, he had re-established himself as the dominant racer on the tour. He smashed McGrath's all-time record of 89 career wins, and appeared to be on his way to another perfect season in the 250cc National class.

But then an old rival, Kevin Windham, came out of a self-imposed exile from the racing world to beat Carmichael at Unadilla and set the stage for another sprint to the finish.

In the 125cc class, defending champion Stewart put himself in a 156-point hole when he missed the first four rounds of the series after crashing out of the Las Vegas 125cc East-West Supercross Shootout. That opened the door for Mike Brown and Red Bull KTM teammates Grant Langston and Ryan Hughes to possibly steal the title away. As the season was winding down, the championship was still up for grabs.

What follows here in the pages of *American Motocross Illustrated: Volume 2* are the incredible photographs made by Simon Cudby throughout the season in an effort to capture the excitement and drama surrounding the most competitive racing circuit in the entire sport: American motocross. ■

The anticipation and excitement that surrounds the start of a supercross season is unmatched in professional sports. It takes a week for a major league stadium that was built for stick-and-ball sports to be transformed into a motorcycle race track; it takes years of hard work and dedication – not to mention extraordinary ability – for an aspiring racer to reach his goal of competing on one of those tracks.

When James "Bubba" Stewart began his professional career, in 2002, many felt that he would bring a whole new level of excitement and diversity to the sport. They were right. In his second season of racing, the 17-year-old Floridian proved that he was no flash in the pan, raising the bar in 125cc supercross with seven wins in nine races and bringing countless new fans to the sport.

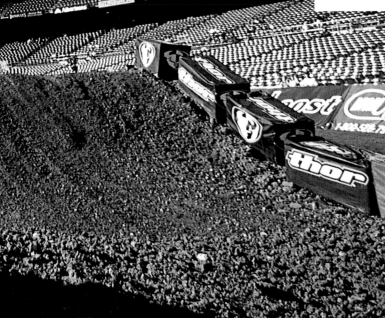

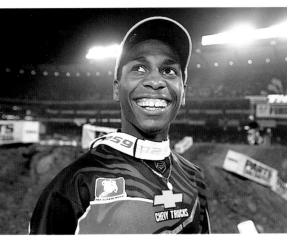

Chad Reed's first full season in 250cc supercross actually began back in October at the 2002 U.S. Open of Supercross, at the MGM Grand in Las Vegas. It was there that he first served notice to incumbent champion Ricky Carmichael that his two-year supercross reign was no longer a given. By the end of the 2003 season, Reed had won more races and was just seven points behind the champ in the final AMA standings.

The leader of the French invasion of U.S. Supercross remains Team Yamaha's David Vuillemin. Nicknamed "Le Cobra" for the way he coils his body around his motorcycle, Vuillemin seemed poised to make a strike at the title (especially after winning the opening round of the THQ/FIM World Supercross GP Series, in Switzerland). Unfortunately, a string of injuries ended his SX season early.

If there was a single race of the THQ/AMA Supercross Series where Ricky Carmichael showed his true speed to the competition, it was Daytona. After taking the lead in the first turn, Carmichael kept the hammer down until the very last lap, by which time he had lapped all of the way up to third place in the 30-man field. It was RC's fourth straight win at his home-state race, tying Jeff Stanton for the all-time record. Who would have ever guessed that Daytona would mark the last main event that Ricky would win in 2003?

F ive of the first six rounds of the U.S. Supercross Series take place in the Golden State of California, the epicenter of American motocross. With the grandstands teeming with moto journalists, photographers, and potential new sponsors, young riders seemingly use every lap they can to try to make a positive impression. Because they never know, from the very first lap of practice to the last lap of the main, if someone is watching them.

Eric Sorby arrived in America from France halfway through the 2002 season. He joined the Pro Circuit Kawasaki team and immediately made a good impression on his U.S. counterparts. But that wasn't always the case in his sophomore season, especially at the second Anaheim race. That's where Sorby got into an unfortunate block-passing battle with defending 125cc West Region Champion Travis Preston. Sorby ended up knocking Preston down and getting fined, but he took full responsibility and even wrote an open apology for his actions. It was a classy move by a top prospect.

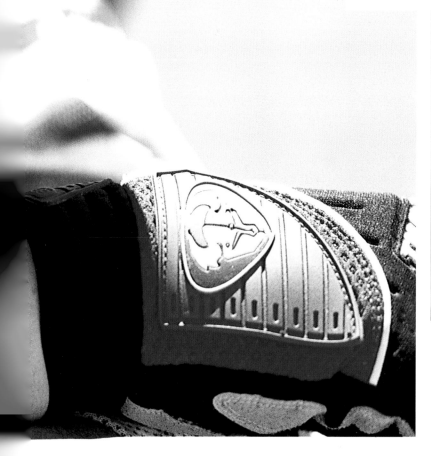

Thirty-year-old veteran Mike Brown led the Pro Circuit Kawasaki attack in the 125cc East Region. Although he has never won a super-cross title, the Piney Flats, Tennessee, native was considered a title favorite from the outset. The former AMA 125cc National Motocross Champion was consistent throughout the series, but he fell seven points short of the title. The highlight of his tour was his first-ever win at the Daytona Supercross.

The young man who held the aforementioned seven-point advantage over Brown in the final rankings was Team SoBe Suzuki's Branden Jesseman. Known almost as much for his quiet demeanor as he is for his impressive speed, Jesseman blitzed to three main event wins in the condensed seven-race championship. He also became the first Pennsylvanian in 26 years to win a title on the professional circuit.

While true works bikes have not been allowed to compete on the THQ/AMA Supercross circuit since 1985, the equipment used today isn't exactly standard. Almost every piece of each race bike is replaced after every event to ensure maximum performance. Every inch of every section of the track counts, which means both the rider and the mechanic must be on top of their game, from start to finish.

The "Production Rule" was meant to close the gap between the haves (factory riders) and the have-nots (privateers). However, with so much outside sponsorship and new satellite teams coming into the sport in recent years, it's getting harder and harder to determine the factory riders from the privateers. But ask anyone in the pits what the single most valuable asset of factory support is, and the overwhelming majority will no doubt answer: works suspension.

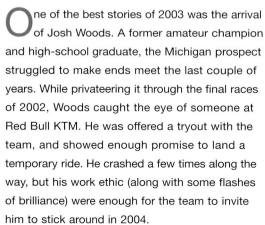

One of the best stories of 2003 was the arrival of Josh Woods. A former amateur champion and high-school graduate, the Michigan prospect struggled to make ends meet the last couple of years. While privateering it through the final races of 2002, Woods caught the eye of someone at Red Bull KTM. He was offered a tryout with the team, and showed enough promise to land a temporary ride. He crashed a few times along the way, but his work ethic (along with some flashes of brilliance) were enough for the team to invite him to stick around in 2004.

Chad Reed may be the only Australian ever to win a supercross main event in the U.S., but his countryman Michael Byrne is not far behind. The Factory Connection Honda rider racked up a pair of fourth-place finishes in the 250cc class before dropping down to the 125cc East Region Series, where he was one of several early favorites for the title. Unfortunately, his tour on the right side of the country was hampered by crashes and injuries, and "Burner" never made it to the winner's circle. Still, many feel it's only a matter of time before Byrne joins Reed at the top.

Georgia's Matt Walker resurrected his career last season with a resounding win at the 2002 Houston Supercross. He and his Pro Circuit Kawasaki bosses hoped that 2003 would see him expand his winning ways, but a few wrong turns – one forced by Travis Preston at the Phoenix SX – plus a late-season injury kept Walker off the top of the box. The tough-talking, hard-charging Walker will be back in 2004, even more focused on making it to the checkered flag first.

N ick Wey is one of those guys who falls into the gray area between being a factory rider and a privateer. Riding for the Mach 1 Motorsports team, Wey enjoyed great support from Yamaha, but it wasn't exactly the full-factory gig he's been working toward his whole life. After a solid fourth-place finish in the final THQ/AMA Supercross rankings, the Michigan native should be expecting a call from one of the "Big Five" factory teams for 2004.

While many are getting paid and supported by factory teams, the vast majority of the riders in the pack are still true privateers. Supercross promoter Clear Channel Entertainment did their best to help those riders, with a myriad of bonus programs from which the privateers could earn more for their efforts. Tops among the independent riders were a couple of old friends from Albuquerque, New Mexico: Keith Johnson (#35) and Ryan Clark (#37).

U.S. Supercross is the melting pot of global motorcycle racing, with riders from all over the world immigrating to the United States for a shot at the big time. But for every rider from Australia, France, South Africa, or anywhere else who earns a spot in a factory big rig, there are ten Americans who are competing for that same coveted job. At the top of the charts is Mach 1 Motorsports' Heath Voss (#28), who survived the long season to finish a remarkable second to Yamaha factory rider Chad Reed in the THQ/FIM World Supercross GP Series.

While his teenaged teammate James "Bubba" Stewart earned the bulk of the attention in the 125cc class, it was Chevy Trucks Kawasaki rider Ezra Lusk who earned the company its first 250cc supercross main event win since Ricky Carmichael bolted for Honda at the end of the 2001 season. After a fantastic duel with Chad Reed, "Yogi" emerged victorious at Phoenix. Celebrating his win with a dive into the Bank One Ballpark pool was his mechanic, Randy Lawrence.

There was no love lost between the two champions of 2003, THQ/AMA Supercross winner Ricky Carmichael and THQ/FIM World Supercross GP titlist Chad Reed. They dug at one another, both on the track and in the pits, setting the stage for a rivalry that should last for years to come. The late-season battles between the two – especially in Dallas and Salt Lake City – will no doubt carry over into the 2004 series.

Coming into the 2003 supercross season, the veteran Mike LaRocco hoped to pick up where he left off when he broke his wrist halfway through the '02 season while still in title contention. Instead, another season of injuries and misfortune kept the 32-year-old legend from Indiana from making it to the podium in THQ/AMA Supercross more than his one appearance there at Anaheim 2. But you can still expect "The Rock" to come out as determined and ready as ever for another run at an elusive supercross title in 2004 – his 17th season on the professional circuit!

Larry Ward is another veteran who keeps coming back for more. In fact, "Big Bird" and Mike LaRocco ended the season tied in all-time appearances in 250cc supercross main events with 189 each. Ward, who rides for the Moto XXX Honda team, completed the domestic series ranked eighth on his CRF450R thumper. He also beat everyone in SXGP.com Holeshot Bonuses by leading three main events from the drop of the gate.

At the other end of the career spectrum from LaRocco and Ward is LaRocco's Factory Connection Honda rookie teammate, Ryan Mills. The New Yorker stood out in a pack of fine teenaged talent in the 125cc East Region. Although he never made it to the podium, Mills showed flashes of brilliance that had many in the press box marking him down for future greatness, but first he needs to keep it on two wheels for the entire race!

Red Bull KTM rider Grant Langston (#111) may have had the most disastrous season of all in 2003. After earning KTM its first-ever 250cc supercross podium, at the Geneva, Switzerland, round of THQ/World Supercross GP, the South African returned to the United States, only to crash out of the first few rounds. His title hopes dashed, he dropped down to the 125cc East Region, only to come up short on a triple jump in practice at the opening round in Minnesota and injure his wrist bad enough to drop out of the series. Faring much better was his teammate Billy Laninovich (#132), who powered his KTM 125SX to fourth overall in the 125cc West Region rankings.

Jeremy McGrath's legacy in the sport of supercross is one of extraordinary success on the track and great popularity off of it. Said Clear Channel Entertainment's Charlie Mancuso of McGrath's importance to the sport, "He has the looks of a movie star, the charisma of a rock star, and he is humble and accessible, unlike most world-class athletes. The records he set in supercross pale in comparison to the impact he had on the motorcycle industry. Those of us that know him are privileged; he is much more than the greatest racer ever."

cGrath's retirement came in the midst of a season of turmoil for supercross. A feud between primary promoter Clear Channel Entertainment and the sanctioning body known as AMA Pro Racing resulted in two series – THQ/FIM World Supercross GP and THQ/AMA Supercross – running simultaneously throughout the season. Although it did not diminish the crowds or the enthusiasm for supercross, it did create an unnecessary tension in the pit area, often leaving the riders and teams in the middle. By the end of the series, there was much optimism for a peaceful resolution to the impasse.

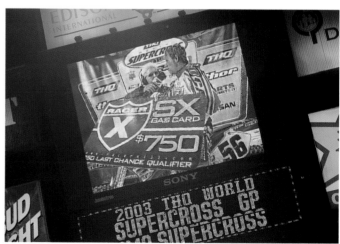

Tim Ferry is the fastest man in the 250cc class to never win a supercross main event. Many felt that 2003 would finally see him break the door down on the exclusive winner's circle, but the Yamaha factory rider from Florida struggled with his comfort and setups on the YZ450F the team assigned to him, even switching back to his YZ250 two-stroke at one point. Just when it looked like "Red Dog" was getting it all figured out, he was diagnosed with the energy-sapping Epstein-Barr virus and forced to the sidelines.

The final supercross of the season, which took place at Sam Boyd Stadium in Las Vegas, could have been an epic battle. The complicated and challenging track laid down by Rich Winkler's Dirt Wurx crew would have lent itself well to a winner-take-all duel between Carmichael and Reed. As it turned out, Carmichael didn't have to win the race to take it all; a third-place finish would suffice. So RC played it safe in second while CR rode to his eighth win in THQ/AMA Supercross. Same time next year, boys?

After five months of working under the lights, American motocross sees a new dawn of sorts when the second season, otherwise known as the AMA/Chevy Trucks National Motocross Championship Series, gets underway in May with a pair of races in California. New faces emerge on the podium and in the pits as everyone starts out even all over again. The size of the pack doubles and race speeds definitely pick up in the great outdoors.

Ryan Hughes is not unfamiliar to American motocross fans. "Ryno" was a top contender throughout the 1990s, but he retired at the end of the 2001 season to teach motocross schools and do some bike testing for companies like KTM. Last fall the team bosses noticed that his lap times were better than those of the actual racers, and he was invited to come out of retirement to race in the 125cc Nationals. By the second race, at Hangtown, he was at the top of the results with an overall win for the first time in eight years. Unfortunately, he broke his leg while taking over the points lead at Southwick and was forced to the sidelines for part of the summer.

As the 2003 supercross season was winding down, Kevin Windham was working on a motocross comeback at his home track in Mississippi. Windham had been MIA from the professional scene for most of the year after his injury, but he had not lost his passion for racing. If anything, he found himself with more desire to compete than he has had in years. And when he finally made his public return at the opening round of the AMA/Chevy Trucks National Motocross Championships at Glen Helen and promptly scored the first moto holeshot, it seemed to put a smile on the face of the entire industry.

It was only fitting that Ricky Carmichael would record the record-breaking 90th win of his career at what he calls his favorite track on the circuit, High Point Raceway in Mt. Morris, Pennsylvania. Carmichael and his family traveled there countless times in his amateur career to compete, and when the Gatorback National in his home state of Florida went away following his win there, he adopted High Point as if it were his backyard race track.

Ernesto Fonseca joined the 250cc class full-time this season at the request of Team Honda. The talented Costa Rican came through with a solid third overall in THQ/AMA Supercross, but he found the going a little tougher in the outdoor nationals. But with Ricky Carmichael running point on his CR250, the bosses at American Honda gave Fonseca and teammate Nathan Ramsey (who missed the entire supercross season with an injury) more time to show their potential with contract extensions.

Pro Circuit Kawasaki rider Eric Sorby seemed to get a new lease on life in American motocross racing when the 125cc Nationals started. The Frenchman was quick to put a tumultuous supercross campaign behind him and focused on getting to the front of the pack. He went 5-4-3-2 in the first motos of the series, just losing the second moto at Hangtown by less than a second. With his inspired outdoor efforts, Sorby was able to prove to everyone that he is the complete package.

With his do-or-die riding style, Factory Connection Honda rider Christopher Gosselaar (#39) always seems like he's giving it everything he has out on the motocross track. He is the polar opposite of the super-smooth Michael Brandes (#68), who rides with such ease that he sometimes appears to be just cruising. Brandes sat out the supercross series but came out firing in the 125cc Nationals, earning a solid fifth overall at the Glen Helen opener.

Another Frenchman showing a renewed dedication once the out-door season started was Steve Boniface. The Red Bull KTM rider did not exactly set the world on fire in his third season of super-cross, but he was definitely going faster in the 125cc Nationals. His third-place finish in the first moto at Budds Creek marked a career high, but would it be enough to keep him on a factory bike come 2004?

And then there was the return of the oft-injured Grant Langston to the 125cc National class. After spending most of supercross – and, like Travis Pastrana, much of the last two years – on the sidelines with injuries, Langston hit the track flying at Glen Helen. His second-moto battle with Mike Brown (#3) was his best U.S. race since his last race win, back at Broome-Tioga in New York in August of 2001.

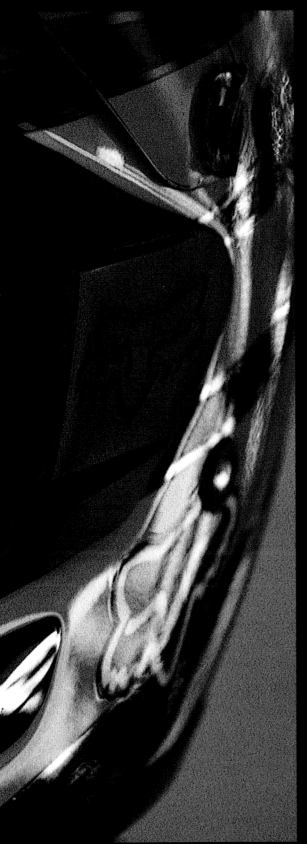

James Stewart's success in his first year and a half on the professional circuit is unmatched in motocross history. In his first 25 races, the Chevy Trucks Kawasaki rider won a mind-boggling 17 of them. The mainstream media began to catch on, too, as Bubba began showing up on late-night talk shows and general-interest sports magazines like *ESPN The Magazine* and the venerable *Sports Illustrated*. Like Bob Hannah, Jeremy McGrath, and Ricky Carmichael before him, Stewart is destined to change the sport forever.

Roger DeCoster's SoBe Suzuki team was once again plagued by injuries, especially in the 250cc ranks. By the time the first month of the season was in the record books, Travis Pastrana (#199) was long gone with a knee injury, as was Sebastien Tortelli. That left Sean Hamblin (#33) alone to carry the yellow flag in the quarter-liter division. He lasted until the fourth round, at Southwick, when he tore up his knee as well.

ike Brown is one of the hardest-working men in motocross. Being Ricky Carmichael's close friend and regular riding partner, he really has no choice in the matter. Week in, week out, RC and Brownie pounded out endless laps together around Carmichael's notoriously rough practice tracks in Florida and Georgia. The hard work paid off, as Brown won (from left, clockwise) the Daytona Supercross, the Glen Helen 125cc National opener, and the pivotal High Point National in the green hills of Pennsylvania.

Factory Connection Honda rider Michael Byrne struggled with his starts throughout the first few rounds of the 125cc National Motocross Series, but he found his technique just in time for Southwick, where starts are more important than they are anywhere else in American motocross. Byrne used those good starts to carry him to his first career win in the opening moto, then into an epic three-way battle for the win in the second that ended when he fell with two laps to go. Shortly thereafter, "Burner" signed a contract with Kawasaki to be James Stewart's 250cc teammate in 2004 and beyond.

While his slightly older and more experienced countrymen Byrne and Chad Reed raced at the front of the pack throughout the season, Australia's Brett Metcalfe spent the 2003 season getting used to the rough-and-tumble U.S. circuits. He enjoyed one podium finish, but fans may remember him more for the high-profile crashes he suffered while battling for a podium spot at the Pontiac 125cc Supercross and the Southwick National.

When Sebastien Tortelli first came to America in 1999 with a pair of FIM World Motocross Championships on his resume, the sky seemed the limit for the talented and charismatic Frenchman. Unfortunately, the years since have been plagued by injuries and misfortune. The 2003 season was the worst yet, as Tortelli needed major surgery on his knee not once, but twice. Like his SoBe Suzuki teammate Travis Pastrana, Tortelli may never get to show team manager Roger DeCoster (left) his true potential.

Sebastien Tortelli wasn't the only rider with rotten luck this season. Privateer hero Robbie Reynard (#17) sat out the entire supercross season in order to be healthy for the outdoor nationals, then hit a course worker in practice at High Point when the man picked the worst possible time to cross the track on an ATV. And Stephane Roncada (#21) was on injured reserve for most of supercross before returning to the 125cc National class. When all of his teammates got hurt, he was moved up to the 250cc division, where he finally pulled it all together for a runner-up finish at Budds Creek.

Veteran privateer Kyle Lewis lost out on most of the entire domestic supercross tour when he tore his thumb up while practicing between Christmas and New Year's Day. He returned in time for the start of the AMA/Chevy Trucks 250cc Nationals, where he finished in the top five overall the previous season. Unfortunately, the time off showed in Lewis' results, as he was struggling to reach the top ten in the rankings at the halfway mark in the 12-race series.

Chemistry is an important part of any team's success, but by the halfway point of the summer motocross season, the friendship between Yamaha's Tim Ferry (#15) and Chad Reed had dissolved completely. They got into a shouting match during practice at Budds Creek, and when Ferry emerged victorious in the first moto, he made sure to let his former friend and neighbor know just who was number one (sort of).

Two of the oldest men in the 250cc class continued to run toward the front of the pack in the 250cc class. Cernics.com KTM rider John Dowd suffered two DNFs when his bike failed to ignite while on the starting gate, but it all came together at his beloved Southwick track, where he finished a solid second overall to match KTM's best-ever finish in an AMA 250cc National. As for LaRocco (#5), he was back on a CR250 for the summer, having spent last summer on the thumper, but he started slow as a result of missing most of the supercross season with a shoulder injury.

Ever wonder what happened to four-time AMA National MX Champion Mike Kiedrowski? How about top privateer Fred Andrews, or even 250cc Grand Prix contender Rodney Smith? Old motocrossers never die – they join the Grand National Cross Country Series! With four-time GNCC Champion Rodney Smith (#1) leading the way, the toughest series in the off-road world often looks like a pro motocross national from yesteryear. However, the championship leader going into the summer break was Barry Hawk (left), who cut his racing teeth on ATVs, not dirt bikes.

Meanwhile, over at the foam pits, Carey Hart was one of seemingly countless freestylers trying to tame the trick he first conquered but never quite got comfortable with: the backflip. After watching the likes of Mike Metzger, Travis Pastrana, Kenny Bartram, and Caleb Wyatt land the trick safely time and again, the rest of the FMX world – including Hart – was forced to flip or fold.

While everyone calls Mike Metzger the "Godfather of Freestyle Motocross," he prefers "King of the Two-Wheel Deal." And after seeing how quickly he mastered the backflip, as well as how easily he adapted to the nascent sport of Supermoto, it's obvious that either nickname fits just fine.

As for the "King of Super-cross," Jeremy McGrath spent his first year of retirement getting his own arms wrapped around some new forms of racing. He accepted an invitation to compete in the Toyota Celebrity Grand Prix at Long Beach, where he turned the fastest laps of the day, then he went wide-open into the fledgling AMA/Red Bull Supermoto Series, hooking up with Jeff Ward and Troy Lee on Team Troy Lee Designs.

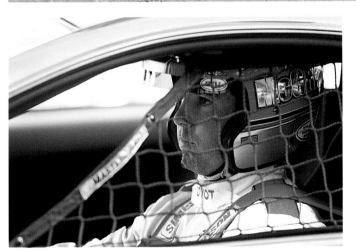

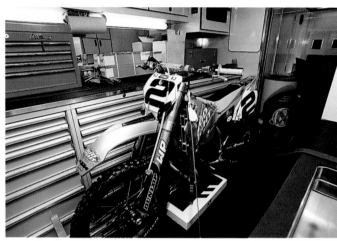

Motocross has come a long way in the last decade. For factory riders and their mechanics, the days of box vans and week-long road trips are long gone, thanks to the arrival of the big rigs in the pro pits. Now most mechanics fly back and forth to each race, just like the riders, allowing them to focus more on the task at hand. One thing that hasn't changed is the fact that he who has the most talent and heart combined (right) usually comes out on top.

While the outdoor national schedule has pretty much remained the same for the past few years, the THQ/AMA Supercross Series made a switch in 2003. New to the schedule was San Francisco's Pac Bell Stadium, which replaced the New Orleans Superdome. The event marked the first time a supercross race has been held in the Bay Area since the 1995 San Jose Supercross, which was won by Jeremy McGrath. Nearly 45,000 people attended the SFSX debut, which means it will no doubt remain on the schedule for years to come.

The latest trend in rider comfort is the personal bus. With the events becoming more crowded and travel across the country becoming more difficult in the last couple of years, many riders are opting to spend their time between and during race weekends in a private motor home. It cuts down on airport lines and lets the riders get more sleep, rather than spending so much time shuttling back and forth between hotels. It was just that kind of setup that inspired new father Kevin Windham to return to the circuit with his wife, Dottie, and baby girl, Madelyn, in tow.

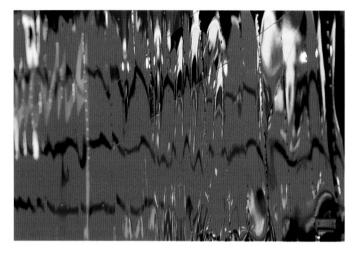

One of the most popular riders on the circuit is Factory Connection Honda's Travis Preston. The former privateer came out of the pack to win the 2002 AMA 125cc West Region title over James Stewart, then proved that it was no fluke by winning the season-opener at Anaheim. Unfortunately, a few mishaps in traffic on the race track as well as a mid-season knee injury mean that he will have to surrender the #1 plate he wore so proudly in 2003.

Yamaha of Troy's Ivan Tedesco saw his stock go up on the super-cross circuit when he won his first-ever 125cc main event in Pontiac. The Yamaha of Troy rider also put in a few top outdoor national finishes, all of which led to the Albuquerque product becoming one of the hot prospects during the preseason signing period. With a well-rounded game and the ability to go fast on any size motorcycle, the best results for "Hot Sauce" may still be ahead of him.

In only his second year of supercross, James Stewart pushed his star even higher into the sky with his dominant wins and unscripted celebrations. He kissed the ground after one win; he moonwalked on the podium after another. By the end of the season, many were looking forward to seeing the soon-to-be-18-year-old joining the ranks of the 250 class in 2004 in order to battle with the biggest stars of all, Carmichael and Reed.

Thousands of young athletes begin racing motocross as kids in the hopes of one day reaching the very top. They come from all sorts of places and backgrounds, which makes it impossible to put a finger on who the next big thing might be or where he might come from. For instance, Mike Brown (above right) hails from the middle of stock car country in Tennessee, while Nick Wey (right) is the son of a truck driver from DeWitt, Michigan.

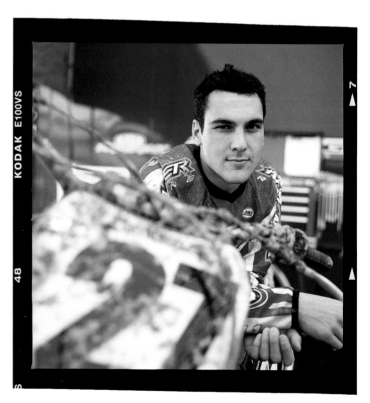

icky Carmichael hails from the Florida Panhandle and has a schoolteacher mother and an electrician father. While all of Ricky's professional wins have come aboard Kawasaki and Honda motorcycles, the first trophies he won as a child came aboard a Yamaha three-wheeler. With the most race wins and the most series championships, RC is now the most successful racer in the history of professional motocross racing.

Mike Brown (#3) and Ryan Hughes (#105) first started battling at Loretta Lynn's back in the late 1980s as schoolboy prospects. Almost fifteen years later, the two were still at it as the 2003 AMA/Chevy Trucks 125cc Nationals were getting started. Their third-round duel at High Point Raceway in Mt. Morris, Pennsylvania, may go down as one of the all-time great battles in U.S. motocross. Over the course of the two 30-minutes-plus-two-laps motos, they were never further apart than they are in these pictures. They split moto wins, with Brown coming out on top, but they will share a great moment in American motocross history forever.

While factory-backed riders like Ricky Carmichael (#4) and Kevin Windham (#14) get the lion's share of the points and prize money in motocross, it's privateer heroes like Solitaire's Ryan Clark who often have to do the heavy lifting. A privateer must find his own bikes, set up his own training and travel schedules, find and fund a mechanic, and then go out there on Sunday and perform. It's a tough and often fruitless existence, but it beats standing on the other side of the fence watching.

Yamaha hired Chad Reed and built him a 2003 YZ250 race bike with the express purpose of usurping Ricky Carmichael as the THQ/AMA Supercross Series Champion. They came within seven points of getting the job done. One unforeseen effect that his late-season supercross charge had was that, by focusing all of their time and attention on catching Ricky indoors, the rider and the team lost valuable testing time for the rapidly approaching outdoor series. As a result, Reed was off the pace in the 250cc Nationals, but he does have all of the momentum going into supercross in 2004.

AMERICAN
## MOTOCROSS
VOLUME 2

When the 2002 season started, Sean Hamblin was an all-but-forgotten privateer searching for a ride on either the U.S. or Canadian motocross circuits. By the time the next season started, he had been inked into Roger DeCoster's starting lineup with the SoBe Suzuki factory team. As Hamblin and "The Man" himself might tell you, hard work and good luck will get you everywhere in motocross.

When it comes down to it, one of the most important relationships in any motorsport is that between a rider and his mechanic. Halfway through the 2003 THQ/AMA Supercross season, the relationship between Ricky Carmichael and his career-long mechanic, Chad Watts, wasn't working anymore, and Watts wanted to get off the road. So longtime Honda tuner Mike Gosselaar was brought in as Ricky's new wrench. Together they held on to the supercross crown that Carmichael first won with Watts, as well as continued his outdoor national winning streak well into summer.

It wasn't too long ago that every top supercross rider seemed to come from the Golden State of California. That's no longer the case, as the Southeastern United States, as well as France and Australia, have emerged as the new hotbeds of factory-level talent. But that's not to say that California doesn't have a few prospects coming up through the ranks, including Juniper Hills' Chris Gosselaar (#39 and right) and Ramona's Billy Laninovich (#132).

Southwick's Motocross 338 has been on the pro tour since 1976. Over the years, the track has hosted everyone from Pierre Karsmakers to Bob "Hurricane" Hannah, from David Bailey to Jo Jo Keller. Each time they visit, the same ruts and bumps show up in seemingly the exact same spots, yet surprise winners continue to emerge from the classic race. It's not just the locals who go fast there; Australia's Craig Anderson won the 125cc National this summer in his first-ever visit to Southwick.

The favorite sons of Southwick remain John Dowd (#16) and Doug Henry (#19). While the older Dowd, who hails from Massachusetts, continues to be a regular threat on the 250cc National circuit, Henry is in semi-retirement at his home in Connecticut. But every year, the three-time AMA National Champion and all-time fan favorite loads up his pickup truck with a Yamaha, puts on his Fox gear and goes to the starting line for the Southwick race. He finished sixth in the first moto this time around, but an early crash the second time out had him loading his bike up before the second moto was over. Of course, after that Henry stayed well past dark to sign every autograph asked of him.

A s mentioned before, Craig Anderson's win at Southwick came in his first-ever visit to the old raceway. While the layout featured several new sections, it was still its rough, nasty self, which should have favored those who have visited often over the years. But a rider who was previously best known to American fans as "Chad Reed's cousin" somehow put together the best race of his life to shock the 125cc National class, as well as himself, with his first-ever win.

ight behind Anderson at Southwick rode his countryman Michael Byrne. Like Ando, Byrne had never won a single moto going into the event. But unlike Anderson, Byrne does not consider himself a sand rider. In fact, the Factory Connection Honda rider seemed genuinely surprised to win the first moto. The fact that he was in contention for the win in the second moto before a late-race fall came as much less of a surprise than the final results, which showed "Ando" and "Burner" giving Australia its first-ever 1-2 in an AMA National.

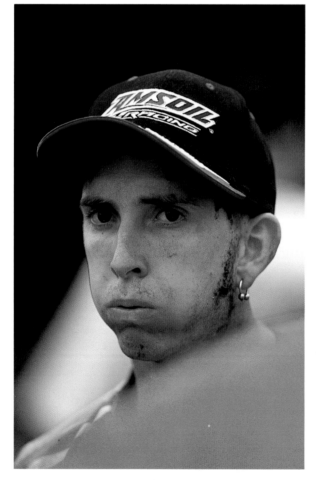

The Southwick National circuit got a makeover for 2003, and so did Brock Sellards (bottom), who ate so much sand off the roosts of Craig Anderson and Michael Byrne in the second moto that it was almost impossible to see the color of his motorcycle, let alone his riding number. Grant Langston (left) and Ivan Tedesco (below) also had their fair shares of problems in the silica of the New England race track.

Craig Anderson (#109) gets out front early as the Southwick faithful watch the start of the 125 National. Before this race, Anderson had been a disappointment for Yamaha of Troy, which imported him from Australia in the hopes that he would be just like his cousin, Chad Reed. But it all came right for the rider and the team at Motocross 338 – a facility known for its underdogs and upsets. Steve Boniface (#55) wasn't so lucky, failing to finish the first moto but coming back for sixth the second time out.

Ryan Hughes has been a motocross folk hero
ever since he got off his broken bike and
pushed it across the finish line at Steel City back
in 1995. After his efforts at Southwick '03, he is
even more of a hero. Hughes broke his leg in the
first moto while running seventh, but somehow
managed to finish the moto in tenth. Showing
more grit than any one man should have, Hughes
taped the leg up, pulled his boot on, and went out
for the second moto. He finished 16th, literally
riding with one leg on the roughest track on the
circuit. It was the stuff of legend.

By definition, Kevin Windham is not a Honda factory rider. However, the support he gets from the company through his satellite Factory Connection team is enough to put him on a level playing field with true Honda factory riders Ricky Carmichael, Ernesto Fonseca, and Nathan Ramsey. With Factory Connection's support, Windham was able to come back even faster than he was before his long hiatus after an injury during the 2002 supercross season.

B eing a pro motocross rider often means living in a fishbowl under the team's awning. Race fans seeking autographs, photographs, handshakes, goggles, or even the shirts off of riders' backs crowd the pits at every stop on the circuit. For David Vuillemin, Andrew Short, and Yamaha of Troy teammates Brock Sellards and Ivan Tedesco, it's all just part of the job.

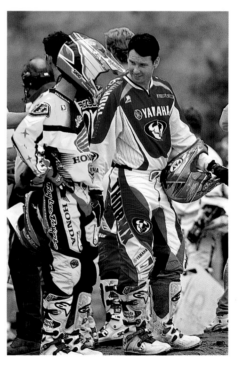

When Tim Ferry (#15) was cutting his teeth as a young privateer on the pro circuit in the early 1990s, Ernesto Fonseca was a minicycle prospect from Costa Rica living in Ferry's Florida neighborhood. Now they are friendly rivals on the AMA National and supercross circuits, Ferry riding for Yamaha and Fonseca under the Team Honda tent. Together, they've come a long way from Bithlo's Motocross World.

When the starting gate is up, everyone is in first place, even in professional motocross. (Or last place, depending on how optimistic/ pessimistic you happen to be.) But once the gate drops, the first frantic turns of any race track have more to do with who wins and who loses than any other part of the race. The winning streaks of Ricky Carmichael (#4) had as much to do with his penchant for avoiding early traffic as they did with his awesome physical conditioning.

Kevin Windham's return to the motocross fold was welcomed by fans all-over the country. After more than a year away from the crucible of racing in order to heal his leg, start a family, and maybe even find himself, K-Dub came back with a renewed desire to compete, as well as that familiar (and perfect) riding style. At his second race back, at Hangtown, he was able to stop Carmichael's 250 National moto wins streak at 26.

WINDHAM WELCOME BACK!! Please throw Me Your Goggles #14

Ricky Carmichael doesn't get the love of as many fans as his success should command, but that doesn't seem to bother him as much as it used to. As the winningest rider in motocross history, Carmichael shouldn't have to explain himself to every fan who feels the need to disparage him from the cheap seats – he can let his record speak for itself.

While the results of the first half of the 250cc National Championship schedule read the same as they did throughout the previous summer – 1.) Ricky Carmichael (HON) – Kevin Windham was definitely making him work for it. Maybe that's because before the series started, Windham said, "If that guy wins every single race this year, you're going to see one mad son of a bitch right here."

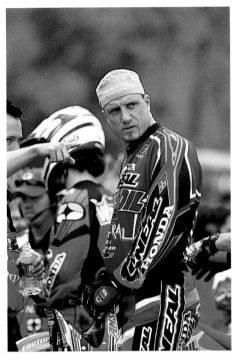

While the desire to win will likely never fade away, the years and the laps seemed to begin taking a toll on the body of veteran Mike LaRocco. By the end of the summer, the word in the pits was that the longtime contender was contemplating a "supercross-only" deal for 2004 and beyond. If LaRocco really did pass them up, AMA National fans would sorely miss one of the all-time greats.

James Stewart's brutal crash at the Las Vegas Supercross had two immediate effects on the sport. First, it proved that even the most naturally talented and confident riders are susceptible to mistakes and injuries. Secondly, it blasted the door wide open for a new AMA 125cc National Motocross Champion. Stewart was forced to miss the first four races with a broken collarbone, more or less knocking the overwhelming favorite out of contention before the series even started.

Before the 2003 THQ/AMA Supercross Series was even decided between Ricky Carmichael and Chad Reed, attention began shifting toward 2004 and the addition of James Stewart to the premier class. Stewart helped light the fire by spending the week of the Daytona SX practicing on a KX250 and laying some very impressive lap times. Although he mentioned racing the first seven races of the coming season on a 250 before dropping down to the 125cc East Region, few believed that they would ever see Stewart ride a 125cc motorcycle again in U.S. supercross.

Occasionally Mother Nature makes her presence felt at motocross and supercross events. (In 2003 she even managed to postpone the Kenworthy's National.) Mud adds a whole new dimension to the races and makes for long hours for mechanics and track workers alike.

Everyone dodged a bullet of sorts at Southwick when thundershowers blanketed New England in the days before the event, but then slackened off come Sunday's race. But practice was still a mess, as Ernesto Fonseca can attest. He was one of the many riders forced to take a "big rig shower" after every venture out onto the race track.

While a series championship once again eluded Yamaha of Troy's Brock Sellards, the Ohio flyer was able to get himself a couple of wins in the 125cc East Region Supercross Series. More importantly, Sellards finally got his health worked out, freeing himself from the clutches of the dreaded Epstein-Barr virus that had plagued him the past few seasons.

Eric Sorby was finally able to endear himself to American motocross fans with his hard-charging efforts in the outdoor nationals. He came to this country halfway through the '02 SX season as a replacement rider for Mitch Payton's Pro Circuit Kawasaki team, Payton having been tipped off by a phone call from Sorby's countryman David Vuillemin. He earned his keep with some good stadium rides, but it was his outdoor results that qualified him for a permanent spot on the Pro Circuit squad.

The Motoworldracing.com Suzuki team has connections all over the world. The team is based in El Cajon, California, is managed by a former pro rider from Colorado, and features riders from both states, as well as Australia, Arizona, and New York. It was the rider from Colorado, Andrew Short, who finally got the team a win when he ran off with the 125cc East/West Shootout at the Las Vegas Supercross in May.

The AMA's 125cc class may be the most competitive division in the entire sport. While the 250cc class is considered the premier division, it has been lorded over by Ricky Carmichael. The smaller division may feature James Stewart at the front much of the time, but riders like veteran Danny Smith (#29) and rookie Ryan Mills (#96) help make up the most intense pack in all of motocross. Whether a rider is passing for first or 21st, he is in for a battle.

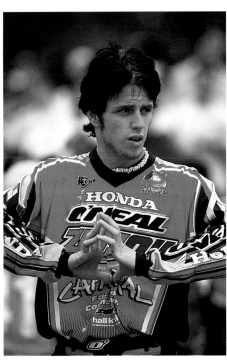

So who is the best supercross rider of all: FIM World Supercross GP #1 Chad Reed or AMA Supercross #1 Ricky Carmichael? It depends on who you ask, though Reed's late-season romp through the last six weeks of the season gave his fans a lot of bench racing ammunition. The 2004 season will start anew in December with the European rounds, and Reed is planning on returning to the continent while Carmichael appears ready to once again pass on the international races. And that may mean another season of two champions but no clear-cut leader of the pack.

Ryan Hughes' return to the 125cc class may have helped turn around what started out as a dismal year for KTM in America. After losing Jeremy McGrath to retirement and Grant Langston to injuries, the Austrian brand's 250cc attack was pretty much nonexistent. And 125cc riders like Steve Boniface, Brett Metcalfe, Josh Woods, and Billy Laninovich struggled to reach the podium. When Hughes won the Hangtown National, it marked the first win of the season for new Red Bull KTM team manager Larry Brooks.

Hughes' arrival under the Red Bull KTM tent also seemed to inspire the rest of the Orangemen to pick up the pace. Grant Langston (#111) battled with Mike Brown (#3) throughout the second moto at Glen Helen to score a moto win and signal to the rest of the class that he was back on the pace after so many injuries. As for Billy Laninovich (#132), he was still recovering from an injury when the 125cc Nationals started and was leaning toward a change of scenery for the following season.

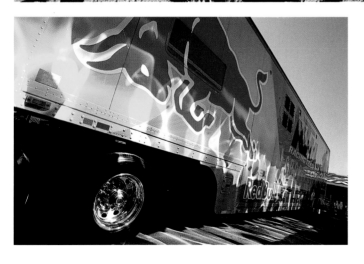

After a long career as a professional motocross racer, David Pingree (#51) decided to hang it up at the end of the 2003 season. The winner of four 125cc supercross main events in his career, Pingree was popular with the fans and his fellow riders. His monthly *Racer X* column, "Electronic Ping", earned him praise for his writing skills and have led him into the next chapter of his life, that of motocross journalist. Pingree, probably the most popular motorcycle rider to come out of Montana since Evel Knievel, should have even more success as a writer than he did as a racer.

The few seconds between the turning of the 30-second board and the drop of the starting gate can seem like forever to a rider sitting on the line for an outdoor national. It is the last time for the next 35 minutes or so that everyone will be this close or this safe, because the moment the gate slams to earth, all hell breaks loose....

A factory rider has the good fortune of having his own mechanic, an endless supply of parts, and the ability to basically ride a brand new race bike every weekend. Such are the perks of being competitive enough to garner the attention and support of companies like Honda, Kawasaki, KTM, Suzuki, and Yamaha.

A Kawasaki factory technician goes over Ezra Lusk's KX250 with a fine-toothed comb after a between-moto power wash. Back in the day, a rider and his mechanic would clean up the bike for the second moto with a wire brush, a scrub bucket, and a screwdriver!

KODAK E100VS    43    3

KODAK E100VS    43    3

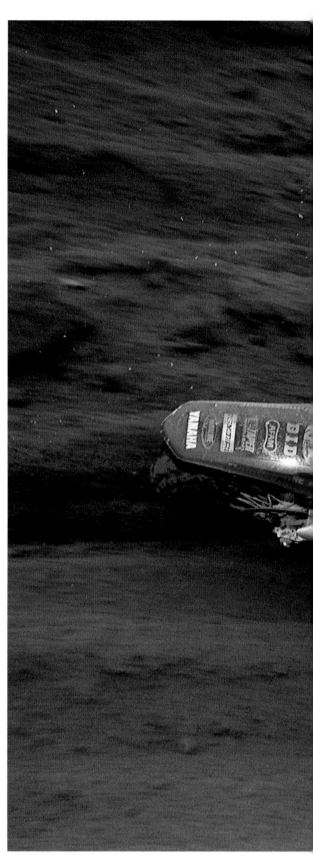

It didn't take long for Chad Reed to position himself as the heir-apparent to his childhood hero, Jeremy McGrath. With his speed, style, and technique, Reed even looks like his idol on the motorcycle. He won his first 250cc supercross main events at a younger age than McGrath, which means that Reed, now just 21, is actually ahead of where Jeremy was at this stage in the game.

James Stewart started his title defense in the 125cc Nationals exactly 156 points down after missing the first eight motos with a broken collarbone. But from the moment he hit the track in Budds Creek, it was apparent that he was far and away the fastest man in the class. At the next round, in Red Bud, Michigan, the 17-year-old simply dominated both motos. Halfway through his sophomore season as a pro, his performances had pit pundits and bench racers moving him ahead of Ricky Carmichael and Mark Barnett on their list of the fastest 125cc riders of all time.

Craig Anderson jumps out of the forest of Southwick, Massachusetts, on his way to the second moto win and the overall. Before that race, the word in the pits was that Anderson was planning on quitting the AMA circuit and returning to his native Australia, effectively tearing up his contract with Yamaha of Troy after a mutual agreement. With his upset win in New England, Ando's future may have reverted back to the original plan.

**K**elly Smith seemed to have the worst luck of all in the 125cc Nationals. The privateer Yamaha rider suffered through a box van full of misfortune, losing out on a couple of podium bids due to mechanical failures. But before the season had ended, Smith was rumored to be in line for a Kawasaki ride of some sort aboard the company's new KX250F thumper for next season.

B efore the summer even started, AMA Pro Racing dropped a bombshell of sorts when they let it be known that four races on the 12-race AMA/Chevy Trucks National Championship schedule may not be part of the series much longer. Among those in jeopardy was High Point Raceway, a facility that has been a prominent stop on the tour since 1977. The event made a bid for itself to remain on the schedule when it went off a few weeks later with a perfect track, under beautiful skies, and before a massive crowd. The same could be said for Glen Helen Raceway in San Bernardino, California.

If you want a glimpse at the future of American motocross, look no further than the AMA/Air Nautiques Amateur National Motocross Championships at Loretta Lynn's. Ever since 1982, the home of the famed country singer has served as the playing field for the largest motocross race in the world. Last year, nearly 18,000 riders tried to qualify for the championship finals, including future Suzuki factory rider Broc Hepler (#54), minicycle sensation Dominic Izzi (below), and Malcolm Stewart (top), the little brother of the all-time winningest rider in Loretta Lynn's history, James Stewart.

Joining the aforementioned Broc Hepler on the Suzuki factory team in 2004 will be Davi Millsaps (#118), who comes out of the same Southeastern amateur hotbed as Ricky Carmichael, Ezra Lusk, Tim Ferry, and James Stewart. The same goes for his Florida neighbor Matt Goerke (#189), the top minicycle rider at Loretta Lynn's in the summer of 2002.

And then there are the Alessi brothers, Jeff (opposite page) and Mike. Together, the two have been prominent figures on the national amateur scene ever since the mid-1990s. In fact, Mike, the oldest boy, was the first rider ever to win a KTM Jr. Supercross Challenge at a round of the THQ/AMA Supercross Series. Now both boys are coming of age in the schoolboy classes with full support from American Honda. By 2005, motocross fans should be seeing these names at outdoor nationals and supercross races everywhere.

A few years behind the Alessi brothers of California come the
Trettel boys from North Carolina, among so many others. The

# J a m e s   S t e w a r t

Ten years ago, Kawasaki's Team Green amateur support manager, Mark Johnson, received a phone call from a Florida man named Purcell Haynes. Purcell was a regular at Florida motocross races: he was the man who dropped the starting gate at Gatorback. A couple of years earlier, Purcell watched his son Tony's promising racing career end as a result of a serious practice crash. Purcell wanted to see if Johnson could help out another young African-American racer from Florida. "We really need to do something with these Stewart folks down here," he said to Johnson. "They're great people, and little James is really something else…."

Shortly thereafter, James "Bubba" Stewart began riding Kawasaki minicycles, and he's been with the green marque ever since. After completing the most dominant amateur racing career in American motocross history in 2001 – Stewart eclipsed Ricky Carmichael's record of 10 AMA Amateur National Championships when he won his eleventh class title at Loretta Lynn's – it was time to turn pro exactly two weeks after his sixteenth birthday. Arguably the most hyped rider ever to exit the amateur ranks, Stewart rode to a strong second-place finish in his first supercross. One week later, in San Diego, he would become the youngest rider ever to win a 125cc SX main event. When he stepped up in front of the ESPN2 cameras that night, he dedicated the race to the aforementioned Tony Haynes – his hero growing up and the reason he wears #259.

As a rookie, Stewart would ultimately go on to win four supercrosses in the AMA 125cc West Region Supercross Series, including another "youngest ever" win at the Dave Coombs Sr. 125cc East/West Shootout in Las Vegas. And eight days later, he became the first rider ever to win his first professional outdoor race, at the season-opening Glen Helen AMA 125cc National.

By the time the 2002 AMA 125cc National Championship was complete, Stewart had won ten nationals, breaking the all-time single-season victory mark – as a rookie! And once again, he went into the

history books as the youngest series champion ever, as well as the first African-American champion in U.S. motocross. But Stewart has never made a big deal of the race issue, his take on the issue being, "We all look the same with our helmets on."

During the winter of 2003, Stewart went back to Florida, where he trained incessantly – and in isolation – for his sophomore season. "I just rode a lot and trained a lot to get ready for the season," said Stewart. "You know, I had a lot of good luck here last year, but I also had a lot of bad luck. I feel really good, the track looks really good, and I think we're going to take it." As a matter of fact, Stewart was planning on taking all of the races in the THQ/AMA 125cc West Region Series – something only Carmichael himself has accomplished in a 125cc SX season.

But after getting a terrible start at the first race at Anaheim, Stewart ran out of time chasing down leader Travis Preston, ending his ambitious plans for an undefeated series.

At the next race, in Phoenix, it was obvious that Stewart wasn't going to dwell on his opening-day defeat. He cleared out early and won going away. "James' ride was just outstanding," said new Chevy Trucks Kawasaki pro team manager Mark Johnson, who was working with Stewart again at Phoenix for the first time since signing him to an amateur contract almost a decade ago. "He's always very smooth and very fluid. Being able to talk to him this week, I could see he's become a very impressive young man. He's quite mature for having just turned 17 years old, and his speed on the race track speaks for itself.

"James loves to make people laugh," added Johnson. "He loves to be able to entertain for people. He can laugh at himself. He likes people to like him. He's perfect for the sport."

The consummate motocross showman, Stewart willingly admits that he's driven by the applause that comes with winning. "Yeah, I like the hype," said the

17-year-old from Haines City, Florida. "I love all of the fans. I think they're the biggest reason why I go fast."

In the ensuing three months, Stewart proved that his preseason plan to win every race wasn't that far off. In fact, after his narrow Anaheim loss to defending series champion Preston, Bubba ran the table over the last seven races to clinch the 125cc West Region title. Then it was on to Las Vegas for another 125cc East/West Shootout.

When the gate dropped, Stewart, wearing the #1W rather than the #259, pulled the holeshot. By the time the first lap was complete, he was three seconds ahead. But a bobble dropped him to fourth, forcing him to mount a charge. Then it happened – Stewart's first big mistake of his career. Jumping out through a difficult triple/double section, Stewart leaned in too much between the jumps and his Kawasaki KX125 bucked out over the handlebars, sending the teenager up over the front end at high speed. Hitting the ground in a sickening thump, Stewart was knocked out cold. As a hushed stadium – including Purcell and Tony Haynes – watched in frightened silence, he was taken away in an ambulance.

Fortunately, he regained consciousness on the way to the hospital. It was determined that he had suffered a serious concussion and a badly broken collarbone.

As expected, Stewart was forced to miss the opening round of the 2003 AMA/Chevy Trucks U.S. 125cc National Championships. In fact, he missed the first four rounds of the series, effectively dooming his title defense before it ever got started, before finally returning to action at Budds Creek, in mid-June. Nonetheless, the perennially smiling Bubba was still rolling with the punches.

"You know, I'm still the same old Bubba; I'm still the same old kid," he said after his Las Vegas mishap. "I'm going to race hard and try and win everything."

Stewart's return at Budds Creek may go down in AMA motocross history as the most impressive performance ever for a 125cc rider. In winning the first moto by almost 45 seconds, Stewart laid down lap times that were faster than those of every man in the 250cc class – including Ricky Carmichael! If that weren't enough, he crashed in the first turn to start the second moto, then passed the other 39 riders in the race within 20 minutes. In one afternoon, he proved that he could win from the front, he could win coming through the pack, and he could ride his 125 as fast as the best 250cc riders in the world.

So fast, so talented, and so determined, Stewart's efforts at Budds Creek and throughout the supercross season sparked a lot of bench-racing sessions over his imminent move into the prestigious 250cc class beginning in 2004.

"I think James racing the 250cc class next year will be interesting," said Chad Reed, the 2003 THQ/FIM World Supercross GP Champion. "Bubba brings some interesting things to the plate. Everyone makes a big deal out of the fact that Ricky Carmichael struggled at first in the class, but I don't think James will struggle. He'll handle it fine. He's been in the limelight all of his life, so being in the limelight in the major class is not really going to change him. It'll be interesting."

When asked how he felt about getting out on a race track with Ricky, Reed, and the rest of the 250cc class, Stewart just smiled and said, "I can't wait!"

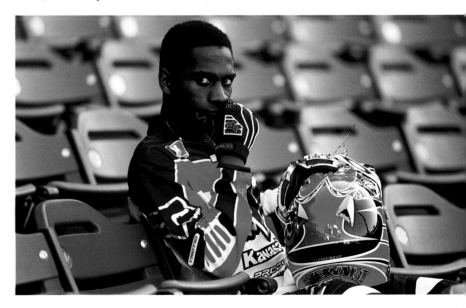

# Ricky Carmichael

The 2003 AMA/THQ Supercross Series was bittersweet for Ricky Carmichael. After a slow start, Carmichael went on a rampage after the third round of the series, winning seven of eight races beginning with the second Anaheim event and punctuating his streak with a dominant performance at Daytona that is already legendary. But, at the very next race, the wheels started to come loose on RC's SX steamroller. After making comprehensive changes to his Honda race bike, Carmichael showed up in St. Louis and was defeated by Chad Reed after a short battle.

That would mark the beginning of a six-race downward spiral where Carmichael (and Honda) struggled to stay with Yamaha's Reed. Throughout the losing skid they tried to get back to where they were with the pre-Daytona bike setup, but they never got it sorted out. However, at the series finale in Las Vegas' Sam Boyd Stadium, Carmichael finished second to Reed – for the sixth straight race – and earned enough points to claim his third straight THQ/AMA Supercross Championship. You could almost hear a sigh of relief from RC when he crossed the finish line, because for him, it was out of the ballyards and back into the great wide open of outdoor motocross.

"It was nice to be out of supercross and move on to the nationals," said Carmichael. "To be honest, I think the outdoors is a little easier for me, and I feel a little more at home on an outdoor track. The last half of the supercross season was pretty tough, and I kind of got flipped around backwards and didn't know where I was.

"The main thing was that I knew I could win the championship, so it was like, Okay, let's just go ahead and get this over with," added the 23-year-old from Havana, Florida. "It's like when you're racing and you have a 20-second lead and you know you're going to win, so let's just go ahead and throw the flag. Your mind just starts going crazy. That's about how I felt.

A lot of guys had been injured, and at the last six races, we all finished in the same place. [Reed, Carmichael, and Ernesto Fonseca went 1-2-3 all six times.] So you kind of knew how everyone was going to do, no matter what the circumstances were. That was the deal."

With supercross over, everyone turned their attention to the AMA/Chevy Trucks National Motocross Championships, which began on Sunday, May 11, 2003, at Glen Helen Raceway, outside of San Bernardino, California. Carmichael immediately returned to his winning ways, not only keeping his record moto-win streak alive at 26, but also reminding those who had come to doubt that he was still the fastest man on the planet.

One week later, though, in the opening moto of the Hangtown Classic near Sacramento, Factory Connection-backed Kevin Windham would snap Carmichael's moto-wins streak as the rejuvenated Honda rider jumped out to an early lead and didn't let go. Carmichael, however, would bounce back to win the second moto and the overall to keep another streak alive: 17 consecutive overall wins.

On Sunday, May 25, 2003, at High Point Raceway in Mt. Morris, Pennsylvania, Carmichael made motocross history by shattering Jeremy McGrath's all-time AMA Pro Racing winning mark of 89 races – a mark thought to be unbreakable just a couple of years ago.

"I wish I could have done it in supercross, because I don't want people to say, 'Oh, well, the only reason he could do it is because of motocross,'" said Carmichael of his 90th career win (33 in 250 supercross and 57 in outdoor motocross). "But you know what? It's a motorcycle race, and everyone has to race the same way. I mean, I can't imagine winning 72 supercrosses, but if you ask Jeremy, I don't think he could imagine how many outdoor nationals I've won. It's like a double-edged sword. We've both been very good at what we do."

McGrath, while quietly disappointed that his record had been broken by a rider who has only been a professional for seven years, was gracious to the new record holder. "It's cool, but it's also weird to think about," said McGrath, who retired from the sport in January. "My record, for me, really, is my supercross record. Sure, I had the most overall wins, but Ricky broke that record. For someone like me – someone who never dreamed of setting records – I'm happy with what I did. But RC deserves to have the record. He works hard; only someone like Ricky was going to be able to break that record."

Bob "Hurricane" Hannah, an American motocross legend who is third on the AMA all-time career win list, is one of Carmichael's biggest admirers. Hannah, like Carmichael, was a rider who had to earn everything he had the hard way: by working his butt off for it.

"It's the RC-Bob Hannah-Jeff Stanton syndrome: You do what you gotta do to win," explained the six-time AMA National Motocross and Supercross Champion. "There are a lot of sissies out there – they do it because it comes easy to them. They don't put the hard work in; they don't have the work ethic. I respect guys like Ricky more than anyone because he used hard work rather than talent to win so many races. It was the same thing for Stanton. He made something from nothing through hard work. He watched everyone, stole what he needed from them, and put it all to use through hard work. You know me – I have no patience for lazy people. Everybody has a lazy side to them; it's just a question of how much of it comes out."

While Hannah missed the window of financial opportunity that today's racers enjoy – he never earned more than a half-million dollars in a year – the Hurricane believes Carmichael genuinely earns the millions he now pulls down each season.

"Ricky deserves every penny," declared Hannah.

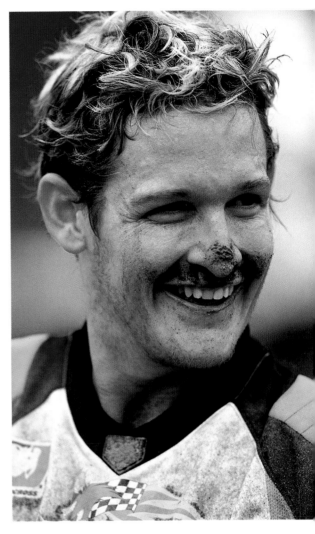

"He should make $10 million a year! Then there are the guys that aren't worth a dime who make $200,000 a year. Who needs them? They show up for the rock star rodeo and make $200,000 a year to finish in 15th place. In my day, if you finished 15th, you ended up working at Burger King!"

In just seven racing seasons, Carmichael has earned a record nine AMA Pro Racing titles (and was closing in on a tenth in the summer nationals) and almost 100 individual race wins. Seemingly capable of always fending off those who dare challenge him, he has allowed himself just a little bit of satisfaction with his accomplishments.

"Yeah, I feel awesome about everything," admitted Carmichael when pressed. "I've won a title in every year of my career, which is something that I can't believe. Myself, the team I've been on, my whole group, my little people, my entourage, we've been through a lot. It's something I could have never imagined back in 1997 when I was just starting out. I think it's one of the things where you don't know what you got until it's gone. I don't want it to be gone. I don't ever want to know that feeling of losing."

# Chad Reed

Chad Reed

"This is as 'American Supercross' as it gets," beamed Chad Reed just moments after winning the THQ/AMA Supercross season-opening race at Anaheim's Edison International Field. "Coming into this race, Jeremy McGrath had just retired, and he was my idol forever. It feels great to finally race and win here at Anaheim, the same place where he always won."

Chad Reed took the longest path conceivable to get to the House That Jeremy Built and to American supercross in general. Hailing from Newcastle, Australia, Reed left his native land in 2001 to race the Europe-based FIM 250cc World Championship Series. But his goal was not necessarily to be the world champion. Rather, it was all an effort to attract attention from across the Atlantic Ocean. He did just that in his rookie season abroad, finishing runner-up to French ace Mickael Pichon and winning the Grand Prix of Belgium along the way. His reward? A ticket to the United States of America to ride for the powerful Yamaha of Troy satellite team.

It didn't take Reed long to display his prowess on the U.S. 125cc stadium circuit. Dispatched to the East Region, Reed rode a YZ250F four-stroke to victory in six of seven races. He also acquitted himself well in a couple of cameo appearances on a YZ250 two-stroke when the series was running in California. Before the supercross season was even finished, word leaked out that the Australian import (by way of Europe) had signed a lucrative contract to ride in 2003 as a full-on Yamaha factory rider.

Before he made it to the winner's circle in Anaheim, Reed traveled back to Europe to compete in the opening two rounds of THQ/FIM World Supercross GP, where he won his first-ever 250cc main event at the second round, in Arnhem, Holland. He finally got a real chance to race with Jeremy McGrath at Anaheim, but two days before the race, eight-time Anaheim 250cc SX winner McGrath announced his retirement.

I was like, Damn, he's done and I won't get to race with him ever again," said Reed of his idol. "At the press conference when he retired, I think I was the only rider that got a little teary-eyed and sort of felt sorry for him. I guess it was like dying a little bit. It was kind of sad." Reed decided to salute McGrath the best way he knew – by winning the season-opener himself and dedicating the win to Jeremy.

From that moment on, Reed dug in for a battle with the man who knocked the supercross crown from McGrath's head two years ago: Ricky Carmichael. Reed and training consultant Jeff Spencer worked diligently to gain ground on the Team Honda terror, but Carmichael's mid-season run of seven wins in eight races gave him a 25-point lead. Reed never gave up, though, and at the Edward James Dome in St. Louis, it all came right for Reed and his Yamaha. The rider found his rhythm again and began clicking off one race win after another.

"I was always just looking to the next race," said Reed of his six-race winning streak, which left him just seven points behind Carmichael for the championship. "On Saturday nights, before I went to bed after each race, I would check out the track map of the next stadium we were going to, which were always next to my bed. So I laid there with the light on, just checking out the track and trying to visualize what it would be like the next Saturday night. I guess I just looked forward to each weekend and trying to keep winning."

Said Spencer, a training and preparation guru who has worked with some of the best riders in the sport's history, not to mention Tour de France legend Lance Armstrong, "Chad's personality and his capacity for creating and executing a solid plan probably most parallels that of Lance Armstrong. They are virtually one and the same people, but in different sports. Self-belief and

confidence come from being prepared. You have to show up at a race knowing you are prepared in every aspect, and Chad has that innate ability to do that. It's not something you can teach; it's part of the person. Chad and Lance share that common thread, the elements which include a commitment to excellence, showing up for duty every day, making professional choices on a consistent basis, the ability to formulate a plan, and being able to size up the competition."

And while Reed could marvel at his own dominance throughout the last two months of the series, as well as his runaway win in THQ/FIM World Supercross GP (where Carmichael did not compete), he was not entirely happy about the way the final rankings read. "I was really bummed out that I lost the supercross championship," lamented Reed after winning the Las Vegas finale. "Now I have to regroup and focus on this one and reset the odometer and kick ass. I want to keep the momentum going. You know, a part of me feels that I got beat in supercross, and supercross is what I love and what I really wanted to win, so I kind of feel I got beat at my own game. I feel the outdoors is definitely Ricky's game, and I'd love to beat him at his own game."

The 2003 season also marked the point at which the Australian earned a significant number of American fans. As he began to win races, he displayed a genuine appreciation for those who cheered him on, which allowed him to win fans over in a way that has eluded previous foreign invaders.

"I have noticed I have a lot more fans, and it makes me feel really good about what I'm doing here," he said as the outdoor national season began. "I could understand if they didn't like me because I was here and taking a paycheck and that was all I was here for, but it's been a dream of mine to be here for so long, and it's so much fun in America. I love living here. I have a house

in Florida and a house in California, and quite honestly, I don't see myself going anywhere else. I'm just happy people take me in and treat me like their own. That's what makes me feel good. This year I was really happy to be myself. I was really happy riding the bike and happy with the team and things like that. This is exactly where I have always wanted to be."

But before you think Reed is going to slow down now that he's satisfied with where he is, think again. "For me, winning is the best feeling of all," he explained. "There's nothing in the world that you can compare to winning. I just love it. It's a drug that you can't get out of your system. You need to get more of it."

And you can bet Chad Reed will be getting a lot more of it beginning in 2004.

## Thanks to:

My wife Sheryl for all your support and for keeping things in line.
My kids Shannon and Callum – nice riding you two!

My parents, and my sister, Lee, for putting up with me.
My nephew Aaran, for being a great video shooter when we go riding.

Everyone at Fox including Greg, Pete, Sandy, Misty, Todd, Dwayne, Scott T., Scrap, Lee, Hye,
Matt, Chip, Warren, Mark (if I forgot anyone, I did say "everyone at Fox"). Brian Price at Shift.

Everyone at *Racer X*, including, but not limited to, and in no specific order, Davey, Langers,
Bryan, Jeff, Julie, Rita, Eric, Chris, Jerri, Jason, Farber, Matt, Scott W., and even Brozik.

Thanks to the best photo-troll in my studio, Ane Morales. Big E – that makes me know.

Ann and Becky from Resource Ink, and Clara, Michael,
and Tommy Lee in Hong Kong – great job again.

John Caper, Bari Waalk, and Shaun Norfolk for Mechanix and Renthal,
and Ted and Anna of course.

Thanks also to Patrick and Alex at Kaos Design for the cool website. Bill, McGoo,
and Drew at Universal. Dave Casella, Steve Blick, Dean Jocic, Kim Boyle and Blair Marlin.
Ken and Michael at Vreeke and Associates. Denny Hartwig, Mark and Sondra Peters,
Sharon Richards, Pat Schutte, Clear Channel, the NPG, and the AMA.

Thanks to all the riders including Ricky Carmichael, Kevin Windham, James Stewart, Mike Brown,
Jeremy McGrath, Ernesto Fonseca, Doug Henry, Ryan Clark, Nick Wey, Sebastien Tortelli,
Stephane Roncada, Kyle Lewis, Larry Ward, David Pingree, Andrew Short, Matt Walker,
Eric Sorby, David Vuillemin, Ivan Tedesco, Ryan Hughes, Grant Langston, Chad Reed.